ISBN 978-1-0881-5512-7

For permissions and other inquiries, please contact the author at author_marie@yahoo.com.

FIRST EDITION

Photo credits:

Front photo: Marie Jefferson Jones

Back Cover:

For Marie's photo: Jay Wackler Photo Studios

For Lisa's photo: Diana Lundin

Cover Design: Marie Jefferson Jones

Table for One, Please: A Girls Guide to Dating Yourself

By: Marie Jefferson Jones

With wisdom added by Lisa Callahan

Introduction: Who the fuck am I and what the hell do I know?

If you are reading this book, you may be recently single. Or long term single. Or not single at all. It may have been an impulse buy, at 3 am on your Amazon account. Or someone may have given this book to you because they loved it. WHY you're here doesn't matter. What matters is that you ARE here. So, now I'm sure you're wondering, "Who the fuck is this chick and what the hell does she know?"

Hi. I'm Marie. When I started writing this book I was 38 and when I finished it I was 40 (who knows how old I am now....lol). I've done a lot of things in my life, but they all centered around helping others. What I hadn't ever done was help myself. I had been married and divorced twice, had a string of bad relationships, and truly didn't know who I was or what I wanted for myself.

After my first divorce, I took a little time to heal, but I never discovered the sheer joy of loving myself. As I started realizing that my second marriage was not right for me either, I started working with a life coach (HIGHLY recommend if you never have). My amazing coach Lisa (who's advice is littered throughout this book like glitter at a girly sleepover) helped me realize that I was never going to be happy in a relationship if I wasn't happy alone. This sounds cliché, because it is, but it is also true.

This book is not about that statement. It's about how to get happy with yourself. I'll let you in on a quick secret....there is not a one size, black and white, clear answer to how to get happy with yourself. Which is why this book is also interactive. I can give you the tools, but you have to do some work. And some self-exploration. And there may be tears (that's ok – I cry a lot). You may get mad at me and put this book down and not come back to it for a month. But I will be here when you are ready. I will help you learn to date yourself.

As you go through this book, I will use some generic examples. Maybe these don't fit for you. If they don't, cross them out and write in whatever fits in your life. Some people like flowers and dinner. Some people don't. Make this book about YOU. There are blank spaces, places to write your answers, and creative spaces for a reason! You are also going to get a lot of stories about my life. I hope that they resonate with you, but I totally get that not all of them will resonate with everyone. Just remember, they are my own personal life experiences and shared to provide reference and example. Not to project how I think your story should turn out or how your story may have been.

XOXO,

Marie, M.A.

P. S. I love, adore, am enamored with, and live on a daily basis the pin up and Rockabilly culture. You will see some of that in this book, and if you aren't familiar with either of those, I highly encourage you to check them out, since they are all about female empowerment and loving yourself in whatever form you currently find yourself.

Ah, Thanks Marie.

Hi, I am Lisa Callahan, CLC. I am a Transformational Life Coach and I know, without a shadow of a doubt, that a woman can have anything she wants to have. She can do anything she wants to do. She can be anything she wants to be, *if* she can start putting herself first and stop letting herself down. I work with successful women who have unfulfilled dreams and I help them create the kick ass life they are fully in love with.

As of this writing I have been married for 25 years and with my husband for 35 years. It hasn't always been easy but one of the ways we have made it through is by having our own interests. I am a Life Coach who loves to work out at the crack of dawn, he is a writer who stays up late watching horror films. We don't have to do everything together. We date ourselves which makes it more fun to date each other.

I have been coaching since 2010 and Marie is my ideal client because she was willing to powerfully show up for herself. She was willing to stretch herself outside her comfort zone and say "yes" even when it was scary. If that sounds like you then we are so happy you are here. Welcome!!

Marie wishes to thank you to the following people:

To Kelly, for showing me how love should be and supporting all my crazy ideas, including painting the front door blue on a random Thursday (and writing books)!

To my momma, Ruth Jefferson, for always being my biggest fan and the world's best counselor!

To my dada, Bill Jones, for pushing me to be my best and giving me great legs!

To Lisa, for helping me realize I knew how to open my own doors and live life on my own terms and helping me find the confidence to do so!

To my bonus dad, Jay Wackler, for taking on a crazy kid that you didn't have to love, but I'm sure glad you do!

To all the restaurants with WiFi in my hometown, especially Applebees, the RedDog Saloon, and Bdubs, for providing food, libations, and internet access away from the distractions of my house (which was essential in the writing process) and to the bartenders and servers (especially Victoria and Guy) in those establishments, your care for me during my writing interludes was indispensable.

To all my friends who shared with me on this journey, the laughter, tears, and fun are what made this book and the writing process worth it!

To my beta readers, thank you for wanting to be among the first to read this book. Your feedback was invaluable and immeasurable in helping me ensure the readability of this book.

Lastly, to all my readers. Thank you for being vulnerable enough to want to buy this book. Thank you for sharing your journey with me. And thank you for wanting to be the best version of you! The world needs you!

Chapter 1: What is dating yourself?

Before I dive into this chapter, I want to start something that will be continued in each chapter of this book. I will be leaving space at the beginning of each chapter for a "check in" and at the end of each chapter for an "ah-ha!" from what you have discovered about yourself. When you fill in these sections, I want you to sit with your check in and your ah-ha! moment each time. I want these to be real, raw, candid, and sincere. I'm going to leave some extra room with each of these sections because I understand that life happens, interruptions happen, and there may be times when working through a chapter takes more than one sitting. And that's ok. That's more than ok. This book is about YOU. And YOU need to work through it in the way that is best for YOU.

◊ Check In ◊ (This is where you write a short - or long - statement about how you are feeling....right.now. I don't want to provide much input as to what to write because I want it to be your feelings, but think about what is going on in your life, starting each chapter of this book, and reflecting on what you are learning as a point to begin. Be honest, be vulnerable, be heartfelt. This is to help you.)

Ok, so let's get started. We all know what dating someone else looks like in our world. Take a minute to write down here what dating someone else looks like to you. Think about the things you physically do, the emotions you feel, the statements you make and those you want to hear. Think about what you may give to the other person and what they may give to you. (Add more writing space if you need.)

____

____

____

____

____

Now I want you to think. Do you ever do those things that you wrote down for yourself? Do you take yourself out to dinner, just you (or order in, if you aren't comfortable going out by yourself – YET)? Do you buy yourself flowers/candy/whatever it is that makes you feel loved? Do you sit with yourself and really listen to your inner monologue and your body? Do you allow yourself to have feelings and validate them to yourself?

If you answered "yes" to all of those questions, congratulations! You are already dating yourself! I hope you continue to work through this book, but I understand if you don't.

If you answered "no" to any or all of those questions (like I'm guessing 95% of you will), then get ready!! You are on the road to being the best relationship you'll ever have! Take a minute, put the book down, go find a mirror, and say (like literally out loud), "THANK YOU," while you are looking deep in your own eyes.

Now that you're back, that kinda felt weird, didn't it? Why is it that looking at ourselves, really looking, not nitpicking what we see, not criticizing our body or clothes or skin or hair, but truly seeing the amazing, majestic, and brave creature in the mirror is so difficult? Truly connecting with yourself should not be uncomfortable or anxiety producing or nerve wracking. But it often is. Why? We want to see perfection and when we don't….we don't want to look at or connect with ourselves anymore.

We hold ourselves to a completely different standard than we hold anyone else. We think things about ourselves that we wouldn't utter aloud to anyone else. We refuse to forgive ourselves for not being perfect, even when we are trying our best. We struggle to see the positive aspects of ourselves and often times refuse to acknowledge them as if positive traits are an all or nothing concept.

I'm not perfect. I am constantly working to better myself, improve areas that I am not happy with, and grow into the woman I want to be. But I love myself in the present. I love who I am on this journey and I love who I was yesterday and who I will be tomorrow. Right now, right this moment, I am the best ME I can be.

When I was 32 I was in a car accident. Over the course of several months of treatment eventually ending in a major back surgery, I gained a lot of weight. I was so unhappy with myself, in my marriage, and in almost every relationship I had. I struggled to see any positivity or light in my life at all. In the year after my back surgery, I ended up losing 100 lbs. I was in the best shape of my adult life. I knew I was comfortable in any clothing I wanted to wear (including bikini swimsuits for the first time as an adult) but I also knew I was still not happy. Not with myself, not in my marriage, and not in other relationships. I was still nitpicking everything about myself, including physical appearance, what I considered my inability to make others in my life happy, and my own interests and hobbies.

At that time, I was also learning that my independence and personal identity were not valued by many others in my life. I changed a lot of things in the year following my weight loss. I got divorced. I moved to a different state. I changed careers. I made new friends and said goodbye to others. I was still not happy. I was still not dating myself.

So, back to what is dating yourself, although we have been working toward the answer in a roundabout way. Dating yourself is all about doing the nice things that you would do for someone you are dating, for yourself. It's going to look different for everyone, because we all give and receive love differently. Let's consider, for a minute, the time when you felt most loved by receiving a romantic gesture. Write it here, and be sure to use words that include all your senses - sight, sound, touch, taste, and smell.

Listen to Lisa!!

When you use all your senses you are associating, really stepping into the experience. So much more powerful than disassociating, which is like watching a movie of your life.

Now that you have relieved the memory when you felt most loved by a romantic gesture, let's think about the time when you felt a romantic gesture that you gave was best received. Again, use words to include all of your senses – sight, sound, touch, taste, and smell.

These two experiences will help you to figure out the way you enjoy giving and receiving love. I get that you might be asking yourself, how does this help me love myself? The short answer is you need to love yourself in ways that you recognize and enjoy. If shopping for something for a partner feels like a chore, then shopping for yourself as part of dating yourself may not be your best bet, even if shopping for yourself is a normally enjoyable activity.

Now, I want you to come up with ideas for ways to show yourself love, basically, ways you can date yourself. For example, I know that I love to receive gifts, but I HATE shopping. I love to receive flowers as a surprise. I also know that I love to fix a nice dinner for someone I love, taking time to set the table, light candles, and create a gourmet meal in a romantic atmosphere. How do I use these to date myself?   I have a florist send me flowers randomly once a month and have a friend who owns a clothing boutique send me a monthly surprise clothing box. Then, within a couple days of the flowers arriving, and on the night that I open my clothing box, I fix myself a gourmet dinner. I set the table. I light candles. I turn on music, generally classical piano, but that's just me. I make sure my flowers are on the table – I tend to move them all over my house to get the max benefit! I savor the cooking process…tasting as I go, drinking a glass of wine, enjoying the music, the smells, the anticipation.

Then comes the date! I put on some nice clothes, do my hair and make-up, and take time to appreciate myself in the mirror. I give myself compliments, making eye contact with myself (sound familiar??) and TRULY believe what I say. And no back handed compliments here. Genuine, real, honest compliments. If you struggle with this part – because it should be included in EVERY date you have with yourself – get your mom, grandma, aunt, best friend, child, whoever, to get you started. It gets easier to come up with the compliments and to look yourself in the eye when you say them, I promise.

After I'm glowing from all my compliments to myself, I go sit down to an amazing meal. I savor each flavor, the texture of the foods, the way the meal flows from appetizer to main dish to dessert. I enjoy my own company, thinking about my dreams, goals, and visions. But I don't allow myself to get too far into my own head. I want to enjoy the food, without distraction. Once I'm replete, I either open my clothing box or watch a movie, new or old favorite. I may go get comfy before this next step, the way you would at the end of a date with someone you feel relaxed with.

Hopefully this insight into one of my own methods of dating myself will help you to determine how you can start, and continue, to date yourself. I want you to look back at the ways you enjoyed giving and receiving love in the past, and use those to write down some ideas for dating yourself. Try to come up with 4 ideas, but if you have to come back to this part, that's ok.

1)____

____

____

2)____

____

____

3)____

____

____

4)____

____

____

Your next step is to literally write down on your calendar – IN INK – the date you will use your first idea. Baring a legit emergency, don't cancel on yourself. Start small, if you need, but these ideas should be bigger than your typical "self-care", so I'm not talking about taking a hot bath and giving yourself a facial, unless you booked a hotel room for the night. *wink wink*

The next step of this chapter is to decide how often you are going to schedule these dates. I recommend one at least every month, but two a month is even better! Write down here your commitment to yourself, whether it is one or two dates a month. Start with "I am committing to myself that I will date myself…." and then you finish the rest!

I want to return to those people you may lean on to help you with your compliments at first. These people are going to be your accountability group, so choose wisely. And from here on, they will be known as your expedition party on this excursion from your every day life. Write down their names here and be sure they are on board to support you on this journey, if they aren't working through this book with you!

Shifting focus a bit, I want to take a minute and talk about some of the side benefits of learning to not only date yourself, but by extension learning to truly love yourself. Two of the most highly rated side benefits of this process are personal identity and boundaries. Finding your personal identity and setting boundaries are imperative to the dating yourself process, as they allow you to truly find your self-image and begin to build your self-worth. And that is what this journey is all about! Dating yourself is about so much more than just fun and treating yourself, although those are important parts of the process. Building a billion dollar self-worth, finding your personal identity, and loving and accepting yourself on this journey called life are other fundamental benefits from the dating yourself process.

Personal identity is who you are, with no one else's input, judgment, or involvement. It is what makes you YOU. It is developed from your interests, your hobbies, your personality, and the things that amuse you. But it's also how you see yourself; your self-image, self-worth, and self-validation. It's your values, beliefs, habits, and principles. I want to work on figuring out what your personal identity is now, and where you might want to take it. Remember, the idea of personal identity is fluid, meaning it is always changing and evolving because you are always changing and evolving.

This next section is going to have spaces for you to write about things that are important to YOU. I don't want you to think about what's important to your family, friends, significant others, or society as a whole, unless it is also important to you. I'm also going to go a little school teacher for a minute and give you my definitions of the things I'm asking you to write about.

Values: beliefs about positive behaviors and qualities that are important to you

List some of the values you hold:

____

____

____

Habit: something that is done regularly and
intentionally but often without deep thought

List some of the habits you have:

____

____

____

____

Beliefs: truths you hold and/or convictions you have

List some of the beliefs you have:

____

____

____

Principles: fundamental truths and/or foundations you have

List some of the principles you have:

____

____

____

____

Interests: things you enjoy doing or being part of

List some of the interests you have:

____

____

____

____

____

Talents: things you have an innate "knack" for or have worked to cultivate

List some of the talents you have:

____

____

____

____

Dreams: those things you want to do, but you haven't put a plan in place to accomplish yet

List some of the dreams you have:

____

____

____

____

Goals: dreams that you have developed a plan to achieve and are putting into action

List some of the goals you have:

____

____

____

____

Now that I made you do all that work, I will explain why it was important. These things that you just wrote down are what make up your personal identity. They are what make you unique and absolutely wonderful. These are the things that you never want to lose or compromise. They may change or evolve over time…but that choice should be yours and yours alone.

On to boundaries. Boundaries are so important in every aspect of your life. They are how we learn to say "NO", how we manage our time and emotions, and how we achieve mutually beneficial relationships. There are 2 different types of boundaries in my world, concrete boundaries and fluid boundaries. Concrete boundaries are those boundaries that cause catastrophic damage to a relationship if they are crossed. For me, a concrete boundary would be physical or emotional abuse in any relationship. Fluid boundaries are those boundaries that change based on your available time, energy, and where you are with your mental health. One fluid boundary I deal with quite often is going out with friends; there are times when I feel up to it, and times I don't.

What concrete boundaries do you hold?

Ø____

Ø____

Ø ____

Ø ____

Ø ____

What fluid boundaries are you aware of in your life?

ζ____

ζ____

ζ____

ζ____

ζ____

Now that we have addressed what comprises your personal identity, made some leaps towards you learning what your personal identity is, and discussed boundaries, it's time to move on to chapter 2 and figure out why dating yourself is important. However, there are several blank pages following this chapter. After you use each of your date ideas, I want you to come back here and write down your experience and how it made you feel, making sure to use those words to include all five senses.

♦ Ah-Ha! ♦ (This is where you write down something that you really connected with in this chapter….that moment that made you really think "wow, that makes so much sense" or "holy shit, thats me" or "omg, what have I been doing to myself" or anything else that you connect with on a deep level!)

Chapter 2: Why date yourself?

____

____

____

____

____

Maybe you feel like this should have been the first chapter of the book. I promise, it makes sense for it to be the second, but you just have to hang in there with me for a few. All will be revealed in good time!

Psychologically speaking, developing a plan can be much easier than determining a 'why'. That's the easy answer to why this chapter is second. The more complex answer will come throughout the chapter, as we dive into why dating yourself is important and YOUR distinctive reasons for wanting to date yourself.

We can't talk about dating ourselves without thinking about why we date other people. It translates loosely to why we need to date ourselves. We date someone else to get to know them. We date someone else to see if we are compatible. We date someone else to discover if we want to keep dating them. How does this apply to dating yourself?

You already know yourself, but do you REALLY know yourself? Do you enjoy your own company? Do you truly know what you like, dislike, and want out of life? You may not be able to get rid of yourself if you find you aren't compatible with yourself – it's a real thing – but you can then take steps to become a person you feel compatible with. Lastly, you will want to keep dating yourself once you start because you'll learn how to truly enjoy your own company and the things you enjoy!

The next thing I want you to do – I warned you this is an interactive book – is to write down your vision of yourself for the future – which from here on will be called your rainbow picket fence vision, instead of a white picket fence vision*. I want you to forget what society, your family, your friends, basically, anyone who is not you, THINKS you need or need to want for happiness. This is all about you.

____

____

____

____

____

*White picket fence visions are those visions that we think we are supposed to want, not the ones we really want.

Take a few minutes and consider that version of you that you just started the process of manifesting (writing it down is your first step to claiming it)! Now, draw and color a picket fence below to match that fabulous version of yourself! (Feel free to trace a picket fence too....my drawing skills are not up to par, but my tracing skills rock!)

I want to add a disclaimer here. There are those people who will be thinking, "This is a book about loving and dating yourself. Why are we talking about things we want to change? Shouldn't I love who I am now?" Those people are correct, in a way. You should love yourself now. But that doesn't mean there can't be things you want to change, improve, and better. Complacency is not a good thing. We need to change, evolve, and grow each day. But we also need to love who we are, who we were, and who we will be.

Jayne Mansfield once spoke of constantly looking to better herself and never being satisfied. You can find the quote on the interwebs. I think it's important to dissect this statement a bit before you jump to judging it (no, I can't read your mind, but I know how I reacted the first time I read it!) There are several definitions and synonyms for the word satisfied. I won't bore you with the definition (there are online dictionaries for that) but I will mention a couple of the synonyms; contented and complacent. When you replace the word satisfied in that quote with one of those words, it is much easier to digest and to see her true meaning.

Part of loving yourself and dating yourself is the knowledge that you are an ever-changing creature. In relationships with others, romantic or platonic, both parties are also ever changing. You aren't the same person you were in high school, middle school, college, or even a year, a month, or a week ago. Loving yourself and dating yourself through these changes is important to your well-being, spiritually, mentally, and physically. We will explore these benefits more in a later chapter, but just know they exist and may be more important than you think!

Now that you have established your rainbow picket fence vision of yourself (and read though my little soap box diatribe), I want you to think about who you are now. Not who others think you are, but who you REALLY are. What do you like to do? What is important to you within your personality (i.e. kindness, honesty, understanding, etc)? Next I want you to make a list below. In the first column, you are going to put who you are today, the good, the bad, and the ugly. In the second column, you are going to put things from your rainbow picket fence version of yourself. Try to align each trait as you list them, matching things you already are with ones from your rainbow picket fence version, but also matching those things that you need to improve with the things from your rainbow version that might be achieved by the improvement.

Here are a couple personal examples from me….(some are things I have worked to change/improve and some are things I'm still working on….remember, I'm not perfect!)

Who I am today	Rainbow picket fence me
<u>Honest</u>	<u>Honest</u>
<u>People pleaser</u>	<u>Being 100% genuine to myself</u>
<u>Kinda afraid to take risks</u>	<u>Unabashed risk taker (within reason)</u>

Who I am today	Rainbow picket fence me
_______________	_______________
_______________	_______________
_______________	_______________
_______________	_______________
_______________	_______________
_______________	_______________
_______________	_______________
_______________	_______________
_______________	_______________

All my life I have struggled with people pleasing. I thought my world would end and I would die of embarrassment if someone didn't like me. (I have since recovered from this malady, but man that was a rough road!) Learning that people pleasing was directly preventing me from living my most authentic life and being my most authentic self was a huge wake up call. I was afraid of the word no, afraid of people not liking me, and afraid of the invisible, yet ever present and super scary, weight of others' expectations.

Finally, a wise, wise person said to me, "Marie, you will ALWAYS be the villain in someone else's story. But no one who really cares about you will make you the villain because you are doing what is best for you." That struck a chord on my heart strings. I started thinking about what was best for me; about why saying no seemed so daunting; about what it means for someone to truly care about me. It took time. I didn't start saying no immediately, but I did start. And I got better at it. Now, I can say no whenever I need to. Without guilt. Without questioning if the person I say no to will be upset.

You may be asking yourself how this will help you discover why dating yourself is important. Or maybe you have it figured out...in which case, please share your figured-outed-ness with the world!

Figuring out who you are and who you want to be is the first step to many things in life. It's absolutely the first step in getting to know yourself in the way that you need to in order to live your best and most authentic life! But why are we talking about it in a book about dating yourself, and more specifically in a chapter about why dating yourself is important? Knowing who you are now and who you want to be is key to determining your why. Maybe you want to become less of a people pleaser, like me. So one the reasons why I made dating myself a priority was to practice doing the things I wanted to do, in the way I wanted to do them.

I'm not saying you need to become a rigid, unbending person to stop being a people pleaser, but working on saying yes to yourself and doing things you enjoy can help you to stop with the "whatever you want to do" or the always saying yes, even when the answer should be no in your relationships with others. Oftentimes, it is much easier to say no to ourselves in the beginning than it is to say no to others. So, tell yourself, "No, I'm not going to reschedule my date with myself. I'm going to do things I want to do, and I'm not going to feel bad for doing it!"

If you haven't caught on yet, I can't tell you exactly why dating yourself is important for you, but I have given you the tools to find your own why. And I want you to write it here.

Listen to Lisa!

Knowing your WHY will help you when things get rough. You can connect back to why you bought this book in the first place, why having a healthy relationship with yourself will change all the other relationships you have for the better.

So you've got your why. You've got your ideas to date yourself and your ideas of who you are now and the you that you want to move towards. Let's talk about another why that is absolutely universal.

Most of you have probably heard of manifesting. If you haven't, manifesting is the art of using your thoughts to attract the things you want and need in life. I'm not saying you can just sit and think of things and they will appear in your life. Your actions have to match your manifestation efforts. The caveat comes in here; when you are actively training your brain to manifest and attract abundance in your life, then your actions elevate to essentially attain that abundance. How does that apply to dating yourself? Here is the answer

No matter your current relationship status, we all want someone in our lives who shows us love in the way that we recognize it. In learning to date yourself, discovering how you show and receive love best, and putting those ideas into practice, you are manifesting a person into your life (or manifesting a conscious effort by someone already in your life) to do those same things. In treating yourself well, you are showing the universe that you recognize your worth and deserve to be treated like the queen you are.

Manifesting isn't easy. It takes conscious effort, time, and a willingness to be uncomfortable. Many of us find it easy to have big dreams, but we are unwilling to do things to attract those dreams into our lives. Imagine wanting to buy a new, high end vehicle. You look at the price, you work out a budget, you struggle to figure out how to make things work. Did you go drive that dream vehicle at the dealership? Did you look at the time or money you are putting towards things that don't help you accomplish your dream of owning that vehicle? Have you spent time visioning the vehicle in your garage or driveway? If not, you haven't done everything possible to manifest it.

That's where this book comes in. Not only will it help you to establish the habit of dating yourself and help you create boundaries that allow you to continue dating yourself, but it will help you train your brain to manifest and attract someone into your life that will treat you the way you deserve to be treated.

What happens if you start the process of dating yourself and you *gasp* don't like it?? We will explore that next!

♦ Ah-Ha! ♦

Chapter 3: What if I don't like dating myself?

◊ Check In ◊

____

____

____

____

____

You may have a current inner monologue that sounds something like this:

> "OMG. I think I'm more nervous about this dating myself stuff than I have ever been before a first date with someone else. I don't know if I can do this. What if I hate dating myself? What if I can't do it? What if I feel weird doing these things for myself? What if I feel irresponsible for taking time for myself away from my family/work/friends/pets/whatever?"

This thought process and inner monologue are not uncommon. I'm going to defer to a concept that I learned from Lisa, who you've gotten to know throughout this book. Lisa taught me about the 'critter brain'. Your critter brain is the part of your brain that encourages you to keep things the same, to ask questions like those above, and to continue to engage in behaviors that aren't the best (also called maladaptive behaviors). The critter brain does this out of concern, however misguided it is. Your critter brain wants to keep you safe. It wants you to stay right where you are because it knows how to keep you safe right where you are. When you start working to change, your critter brain has to change with you and it's SUPER resistant to that change.

Listen to Lisa!

We don't want the critter brain to go away. It is a critical part of surviving but we can ask that it simmer down. The thing is, all the critter brain needs is to see you can survive this new change. That is why keeping your first date with yourself is so important. It might feel weird, but it will be the beginning of a new experience that will eventually calm the critter brain.

Sometimes just knowing about your critter brain can help. Sometimes you have to look at what your critter brain is telling you and ask yourself what the positive intention is behind that silly little critter brain statement. Once you've discovered that positive intention, you can assure your critter that you've got this and that change is good. Maybe that's still not enough. In that case, talking to someone can help. If you are in a romantic relationship, get your significant other on board. If you aren't, talk to another influential person in your life. You don't have to give them all the deets on what you are doing, but there are times when hearing someone else say, "Its ok to take time for you," can be really helpful. The beginning of a journey to find and love yourself is absolutely one of those times.

What happens if you really do hate dating yourself? Easy answer, keep doing it until you don't. It might feel awkward. You may struggle because you aren't the person you thought you were or the person you want to be. This is part of the dating yourself process. Remember the list of attributes we made earlier? Dating yourself allows you to work on building those attributes, incorporating them into your being, and developing yourself into the vision you have for the future you.

But, and this is a big but (and I cannot lie), dating yourself also gives you a chance to love yourself now. Right. Where. You. Are. This is a key part of the process. You need to love you in this very moment, even as you are striving to bloom into this vision of your future self. Think about this concept of blooming. Plants grow and grow and the flowers that everyone loves come last. I would bet that you still love the plant even without the colorful, fragrant blooms. You still take care of it, give it sun and water and fertilizer.

It's the same process with you. Love yourself now. Give yourself sun and water and healthy foods (with some treats added in there – I will never tell anyone to deprive themselves) and healthy thoughts through what? DATING YOURSELF!! Then watch yourself bloom into the beautiful vision you have created.

Dating yourself isn't always easy. Most things that produce change aren't. Change is uncomfortable. Growth is uncomfortable. You're going to learn a lot of things through this process and you may not like some of them. That's where the concept of dating yourself begins to gather steam, chugging along towards a whole, happy, and healthy self.

You don't hesitate to love others through tough situations and times. You don't write someone off because they are working on growing. Humans are messy, challenging, and in no way, shape, or form perfect. And YOU ARE A HUMAN. Give yourself grace. Allow yourself to feel the discomfort as you grow. And love yourself while you are working to bloom.

Let's take a minute to do a little exercise. I want you to pretend that 13 year old you is standing in front of you. I want you to tell that 13 year old who you are right now. Remember, as you answer these questions, that 13 year old KNOWS that she is a younger version of you.

Who are you personally (like in your personal life......as a friend, partner, mother, daughter, etc)?

____

____

____

____

____

Who are you professionally?

____

____

____

____

____

Who are you internally?

____

____

____

____

____

       I would wager a bet that when thinking about talking to your 13-year-old self you are being much kinder than you would be talking to yourself today. Why would we do that? Why would we be kinder to 13-year-old us than we are to ourselves today? Simply, we are programmed by society to uplift and encourage our children, but as an adult we are programmed to see what society dictates as our reality, which no longer includes hopes and dreams, but rather is based on a fictitious formula for happiness.

       Your idea of happiness does not have to match the ideas your neighbor, family, friends, or anyone else have. Your idea of success should be only yours as well. To some, success and happiness is financially based. To others, it is family and friends and relationship based. Most people who truly have a chance to think about where their happiness is based and what constitutes success to them, it is a blend of both.

Let me preface the following questions by that saying that happiness should always be internal. It should never be dependent on someone else. This being said, there are people, places, things, etc. that have the ability to add to your happiness. And that is what I am hoping you will address in the following questions; those things that add to your happiness.

What brings you happiness?

What do you think could add happiness to your life?

Where do you feel you currently have success?

Where would you like to continue to add success in your life?

I hope that the things you wrote were kind to yourself. Any time you find yourself slipping back into a negative thought pattern regarding your goals and dreams or a negative self-talk cycle, I want you to slow down. Stop those thoughts. Take some deep breaths. Then replace those negative thoughts and self-talk with the things you would say to 13-year-old you. Eventually, you will find that you replace those negative thoughts and self-talk subconsciously.

Negative self-talk can be a formidable opponent. But I have some ways to help give it that 1-2 punch combo and send it packing. First, you have to be conscious of the negative self-talk. This is usually the most difficult part of ridding your brain of this negative pattern. For me, most of my negative self-talk was centered around looking in the mirror. I started really concentrating on the thoughts I had whenever I was looking in the mirror. I began to recognise those negative self-talk thoughts.

After I began to recognize the thoughts that needed to be replaced, I had to decide what new, positive self-talk to replace them with. This can be a difficult step, but using that idea of talking to the 13-year-old you tends to make it easier. I really like writing things down (in case you haven't noticed) so I made a list. For each negative self-talk thought I wrote down, I countered it with a positive self-talk thought. Then I went one step further. I started writing those positive self-talk statements on sticky notes. I left them everywhere. I also wrote those positive self-talk statements on my bathroom mirror in dry erase marker (since that is where much of my negative self-talk took place). By keeping those positive self-talk statements in front of me on a daily basis, I slowly began to subconsciously replace the negative self-talk with the positive self-talk.

Below, write down your negative self-talk, replacement positive self-talk, and some of your ideas to help replace your negative self-talk with positive self-talk.

<u>Negative</u>   <u>Positive Replacement</u>

________________   ________________

________________   ________________

________________   ________________

________________   ________________

________________   ________________

________________   ________________

________________   ________________

________________   ________________

<u>Ideas to help with the replacement</u>

As you begin to tackle the negative self-talk, you will see significant changes come into your life from this one, fairly simple task. They may be difficult for you to notice at first, but those around you should be able to share with you what they notice!

♦ Ah-Ha! ♦

◊ Check In ◊

____

____

____

____

____

     Based on the title of this chapter, you may be thinking it will be an easy one. Think again! Learning how to truly, genuinely, wholeheartedly date yourself when you are single isn't an easy task. It takes thought, time, consistency, and a willingness to step out of your comfort zone. In the end, however, you will develop an authentic joy for spoiling yourself, an honest love for your own company, and an indisputable desire to continue dating yourself for the rest of your life.

     For those readers who are currently not single, DON'T SKIP THIS CHAPTER!!!! You may think it won't apply to you, but many of the ideas from this chapter will carry over into the next chapter where we will discuss dating yourself when you are dating someone else (or married to them). Also, you never know which of your single friends may need advice (I would suggest buying them this book….lol) and this chapter will be full of ideas you can share.

What does dating yourself when you are single entail? The simple answer is it encompasses taking all the ideas from the first few chapters of this book and putting them together. The not so simple answer is that it entails shifting your mindset into a place where doing things for your mental, physical, and spiritual well-being are forefront in your thought process. It involves making yourself a priority – EVERY DAMN DAY – but especially on the days when you actively date yourself (implementing those ideas we discussed in chapter 1).

We consistently prioritize others before ourselves. We are taught that we are supposed to do that and by prioritizing others before ourselves, we are showing them how much we love them. In reality, if you are not prioritizing yourself, you can't sincerely and adequately prioritize and love someone else. Pretty much everyone I know, so I would assume most of you as well, has heard the quote, "You can't pour from an empty cup," but I want to take that a step further. And since I'm extra, instead of saying things about pouring from a cup, we are going to use a goblet.

You cannot allow your goblet to get so empty that you are pouring the last little bit into someone else's drinking vessel. You need to be filling your goblet on a daily basis by doing small things.

Listen to Lisa!

I'll take Marie's analogy even further. Not only should you not be pouring from an empty goblet, should should only be pouring from the overflow. Your goblet should always be full, only then can you be helpful to others.

So, where does this overflow come from? Your bottle. And you fill that bottle by doing the big date ideas every other week or once a month. By ensuring that you always keep that bottle and goblet full, you will never be giving the last of yourself to someone else. And that is what keeps you sane and able to function as a partner, parent, friend, daughter, etc.

This seems like a good place to write some stuff down…..like the name of the bottle you're working to re-up on your date yourself nights. Maybe you can also name your goblet, and color it whatever fabulous, fancy colors you desire! (Again, draw or trace a goblet and bottle here! Then fancy them up!)

Now that we have let our creative selves come out and had some fun naming the bottle and drawing and coloring things, let's talk about how to make sure we are filling our goblet on a daily basis and filling that bottle at least once a month. To begin this discussion, we need to address why it is so important that we fill our goblet daily and never let it get empty.

I'm going to use a real life example from my own story to begin. Prior to discovering how important it is to date myself, I was a give, give, giver. I thought that I always needed to be doing, helping, providing, contributing, and sacrificing of myself. I have always devoted my professional life to the art of giving, first as a nurse (and now as a therapist). Let's go back to 2014. I was working LOTS of hours as a nurse, taking care of patients who were having or had recently had surgery. In addition, as my nurse readers know, you take care of the doctors you work with and other staff members, because as a nurse, that is what you are trained to do; to care for others.

I was desperately unhappy personally. I never was able to take time for me. Not only did I not take time for me, but I had begun a very detrimental inner monologue about myself. I didn't speak words of kindness and hope to myself, instead I was consistently cutting myself down. My goblet was completely empty, dry, and I had thrown my bottle in the trash. I started to get burnt out at work. I was not the nurse I wanted to be. I was not the woman I wanted to be. I was not the friend I wanted to be.

I kept trying to fit into groups where I knew I didn't really fit. I didn't understand that I didn't have to be someone else to be accepted; that I didn't have to change to have friends. I kept trying and trying and trying. I never had that tribe. Never felt like I had a group of friends that I could always count on. Don't get me wrong, I had some great friends during this time. But they were far away so I didn't have that close relationship I was longing for with them.

I could never figure out why I couldn't be the person I knew was inside of me. I got more and more frustrated and spiraled down into a depression. I knew I needed to make changes, but I didn't know what adjustments needed to happen. So I tried giving more, even though I didn't have any more to give. And the cycle just perpetuated. Finally, I took some time for me. During my little retreat, I discovered that my goblet was dry and my bottle was gone. I still wasn't sure how to fill them, but what I did know told me that what I was doing was clearly not working. I made some personal and professional adjustments. I got divorced. I changed my career path and went back to school. I started looking for more organic friendships, rooted more in shared experiences and commonalities other than proximity.

While these things were positive, I still was not making the transformation that I knew I needed. I continued to strive for the life I knew I could have and made minor modifications, but still never developed to the potential I KNEW was inside of me. I spent years and years looking for ways to get that person and potential to come to the surface. I wasted time, energy, money, and emotion attempting to unleash the chains. Little did I know, I had the keys to those locks the whole time.

Enter Lisa, a few years later. After our first conversation, I knew that she was going to help me discover how to revolutionize my life. That's the amazing thing about working with a life coach. Lisa never told me what to do, instead she helped me realize what I needed to do. And one of those things was that I needed to date myself, invest in myself, empower myself.

I started small, doing things to pamper myself. I learned that "No" is a complete sentence and I didn't owe anyone an explanation as to why I was saying no. I quickly noted that the small things would help me for a day or two, but they weren't the long-term solution I was seeking. As a result, I started doing bigger and bigger things. Interspersing these big things with the small daily self-care led me to notice that I was more successful personally and professionally. I was attracting others into my life that were uplifting, prosperous, and flourishing. I had a direction professionally that I had never imagined would be a possibility.

This point in my life was where I realized I needed to share what I had learned. I wanted to help others who are trying to pour from an empty goblet. I wanted to change the mindset that many people have regarding putting themselves last on their priority list. I wanted to inspire YOU to truly indulge, to treasure spending time, effort, and money on your own wellbeing, and to learn that pampering yourself is not a luxury, but a necessity.

I share that story for several purposes. First, don't be hateful to yourself if you've been trying to pour from an empty goblet. I'd wager a bet that you either didn't know that your goblet was perpetually empty or that you didn't know what to do to fill it. Second, I want every single one of you to know that I had to learn this dating yourself thing too. I wasn't doing this from the get-go, it took me concerted time and effort to learn how to date myself. Of course, I didn't have a guide like this to help me. Third, and lastly, I want you to know that I believe, seriously and honestly BELIEVE, that you can fill your goblet and your bottle and live your life the way you were meant to and the way you want to!

I want you to think about where you are in this moment and truthfully answer these questions.

Is your goblet full? Empty? Somewhere in between?

____

Do you have a bottle?

____

If so, how much is in it?

____

Now that we have identified your current goblet and bottle situation, let's dive into the difference between the two. Your goblet contains the amount of energy, time, and emotion you have <u>each day</u> to give to others AND to yourself. This is why you don't ever want to pour the last of what's in your goblet into someone else's. Your bottle contains your reserve energy, time, and emotion for <u>the month</u> (or two weeks, if you determined earlier that you want to do two big dates a month for yourself). This is why, when we need to fill our bottle, the gesture to our self-love and self-care needs to be bigger than what we do on a daily basis. We need to recharge, recoup, and regenerate that energy, time, and emotion for 2-4 weeks of use by ourselves and others.

I want to help you explore both the big date ideas to refill your bottle, but also the daily, small self-kindnesses that you can use to replenish your goblet. The goal in all of this is to NEVER have an empty goblet or bottle. Now, we get to do more fun stuff! I'm going to share some of my personal big date ideas and some of my daily self-kindness, but I highly encourage you to come up with your own ideas! From here on, we will call the daily things Everyday Dates and the other monthly/biweekly dates the Big Dates.

My Personal Everyday Dates

Þ Taking a long bubble bath with a good book and a glass of wine

Þ Taking a walk around the neighborhood listening to music

Þ Spending at least half an hour snuggling with my dog and/or cat without worrying about the time

Þ Spending at least an hour reading without worrying about the time

Þ Watching one of my favorite "guilty pleasure" movies or TV shows in bed (no matter what time it is)

Þ Getting a fancy coffee or drink and people watching for an hour

Þ Getting a massage

Þ Unplugging from technology for a whole evening

My Personal Big Dates

Þ Having flowers sent to me randomly once a month

Þ Having a monthly subscription service (clothing, makeup, anything else you're excited about)

þ Fixing myself a nice dinner complete with candles and wine/bourbon

þ Going to a day spa for a full treatment

þ Taking a weekend away in a hotel/rental cabin

þ Taking myself to dinner and a movie

þ Going to the nearest mall and window shopping (well, mostly window shopping…lol)

You'll notice that there are a lot more ideas for the Everyday Dates than for the Big Dates. I'm sure you can reason that out in your head, but just in case you are not seeing the big picture, you will be doing more of the Everyday Dates since they are something you will do every day or every other day.

We have now arrived at the part where you get to write down your ideas for dates! I'm including 10 lines for the Everyday Dates and 5 for the Big Dates, but feel free to come up with as many as you want!

<u>Your Everyday Dates</u>

þ ____________________________________

____

þ ____________________________________

____

þ ____________________________________

____

þ ____________________________________

þ ______________________________

þ ______________________________

þ ______________________________

þ ______________________________

þ ______________________________

Your Big Dates

þ ______________________________

þ ______________________________

þ ______________________________

þ ______________________________

þ _______________________________________

You may be thinking, "Ok, so I have these ideas, but what do I do with them?" Simply, you do them! But I understand that isn't as simple as it seems. You may need accountability to make sure you are dating yourself and that's ok. Find a friend who wants to make changes in their life. Call on a trusted family member. Tell a random person on social media that you know will hold you to your plans. WRITE YOUR PLANS ON YOUR CALENDAR IN INK!!!! Do whatever is needed as you are starting out to gain the accountability required so you do these things for YOU. Eventually, doing these things to date yourself will become second nature and then you can give accountability to someone else! Use the next space to write down some people who can give you that accountability.

☺ _______________________________________

☺ _______________________________________

☺ _______________________________________

☺ _______________________________________

☺ _______________________________________

☺ _______________________________________

♦ Ah-Ha! ♦

Chapter 5: How does dating yourself help you date someone else?

In our last chapter we talked about what dating yourself looks like when you are single; the ins and outs of treating yourself like a queen (because you are) and the ebb and flow of ensuring you are always mindful of keeping your goblet and bottle filled. That brings us to what dating yourself does to help you date someone else – and I will continue to refer to any relationship with your significant other as dating because even in marriage or a long term committed relationship continuing to date each other, and yourself, is imperative.

Does dating yourself really help you date someone else? Short answer, HELL YES. Of course, I can't just leave it at that. Therefore, here comes the long answer. Dating yourself does several things for YOU, but it also can help your significant other. First let's get down and dirty with what dating yourself does for you, regarding dating someone else.

First, dating yourself allows you to explore **your** interests and things that **you** enjoy. When you are dating someone else, those independent interests and hobbies become very important. Maintaining individuality in a relationship is crucial as it allows for you and your significant other to continue filling your own bottles and goblets, it can prevent the relationship from becoming stagnant, and it allows you to maintain your own personal identity. You might want to underline, highlight, or otherwise emphasize this next sentence.

> Just because you become identified as a part of a relationship, does not mean that you lose your personal identity. It should continue to shine through just as much as your joint identity. Your joint identity should help to boost and highlight your personal identity, much like how complementary colors work.

Maintaining your personal identity and your boundaries surrounding that identity is unbelievably vital. This brings us to the second way that dating yourself helps you date someone else. I want to start by saying that the meaning of personal identity in this book and context is a identity you have developed full of interests, hobbies, and pursuits that are positive and not harmful to yourself or anyone else. Your personal identity should also be just that, personal. Its not things that you do with your partner. As that is now cleared up, lets get on to my second point.

Partners who do not respect your boundaries regarding personal identity are not true partners. Someone who wants you to lose your identity isn't interested in what is best for you. They are interested in what is best for them and in many cases that leads to a relationship that is not fulfilling but also has the risk of being negligent or abusive. Since you've already committed to dating yourself, shaping that personal identity, and setting those boundaries, you've started the process of developing a habit that can draw attention to potential red flags in other relationships. Anyone who truly wants a relationship with you would never ask you to change who you are or want you to nullify your personal identity.

Boundaries are hard. There is no other way to say that. And, for complete transparency, I still struggle most with boundaries. But I know I struggle. So I ask for accountability from several people. And they all have permission to keep tabs on my progress and my mindset regarding dating myself.

The third way that dating yourself can help when you are dating someone else is that it provides an example of what makes you feel loved. If your monthly self-date includes flowers and dinner, then your partner will know that bringing you flowers and dinner (or taking you to dinner) will be a way to show they care. On the reverse, dating yourself also improves your awareness of things that make others feel loved. That awareness can exponentially impact your ability to show love to your partner. Dating yourself can also foster discussion about the way you and your partner show love and feel loved.

Lastly, dating yourself helps you date someone else because it retrains your brain to discover, cherish, and appreciate the time and energy that is being spent on you by your significant other and the opposite, by you on your significant other. At the beginning of a relationship, we attach significant importance to making our partner feel wanted and loved. Then months and years go by, and life happens, and maybe we don't spend as much time doing those things to make them feel wanted and loved.

When you retrain your brain by doing those things for yourself, it also allows your brain to quickly pick up on times when you need to do those things for others. It's kind of like learning to drive. You start out on streets that aren't as populated, learning how to control the vehicle, how to respond in various situations, and then progress to busier streets and finally to interstate driving. Retraining your brain works very similarly. By starting with a process that has intrinsic personal value (dating yourself), your brain is then primed to add more roadways that come with increased traffic (dating someone else).

Listen to Lisa!

What Marie is describing here is an anchor. We all know that an anchor is what keeps a boat moored in rough waters. A personal anchor, like a picture, an index card, a song, can keep you moored to why you want to date yourself even if things get rough. I usually invite my clients to pick an anchor for each sense: sight, sound, touch, taste and smell, so they have lots of options.

Let's look at those anchor ideas and choose something for each of the senses. I want you to list your anchor item and why you chose it.

<u>Anchor</u>   <u>Why??</u>

Sight: _________________   _______________________

____

____

____

<u>Anchor</u>   <u>Why??</u>

Sound: _______________   ___________________________

                              ____

                              ____

                              ____

Touch: _______________   ___________________________

                              ____

                              ____

                              ____

Taste: _______________   ___________________________

                              ____

                              ____

                              ____

Smell: _______________   ___________________________

                              ____

                              ____

                              ____

      Be sure that your anchors are things you can carry with you or at least carry a symbol of them with you. Having anchors can be so important to centering yourself when things get difficult in creating the life you want and the relationship you desire to have with yourself.

Now that we have discussed how dating yourself helps you date someone else, its time to dive into the whys of continuing to date yourself even when you are in a relationship. But first, I want you to list some "I am" statements below. These are going to be important in a future chapter, but I think this is the right time for you to think about those strengths you possess.

I am _____________________.

I am _____________________.

I am _____________________.

I am _____________________.

I am _____________________.

I am _____________________.

I am _____________________.

I am _____________________.

◆ Ah-Ha! ◆

Chapter 6: Do I have to continue dating myself once I start dating someone else?

◊ Check In ◊

____

____

____

____

____

Y'all know by now how much I love my short and long answers. I'm guessing you know the short answer already, but in case you don't, YES, you need to continue dating yourself when you date someone else. The long answer builds further on the discussion from the last chapter.

We already discussed how dating yourself helps you date someone else, but WHY is that important? Boundaries, yes, we hit on those a bit. Retraining your brain, of course, we hit on that as well. So there have to be more WHY'S to this puzzle, right? Of course there are! This chapter is going to help you figure out your WHY regarding the importance of continuing to date yourself once you are dating someone else.

In Chapter 2 we explored your WHY for dating yourself. The WHY of continuing to date yourself will directly correlate to your WHY from Chapter 2, but we are going to expand it further. Just so you have it close by (and have to write it again), let's get your WHY from Chapter 2 down here.

____

____

____

____

Now that you remember why you want to date yourself, I'm going to hit on some tough questions about your past relationships (and current – if you aren't single). I want you to think back to your last 2 relationships, or your current and most recent past relationship to answer these questions. And please, PLEASE, be as truthful as possible with yourself. It only hinders your own progress if you are not. I will use 2 different symbols for the 2 relationships so you can keep your answers organized.

You can keep your answers to these questions short. We will further explore them later, but for now, simple is better.

Question 1: In your relationships, have you ever maintained your own interests and hobbies (this doesn't count work)?

..
____

§ _______________________________________

Question 2: In your relationships, have you ever felt smothered or like things are stagnant?

..
____

§ _______________________________________

Question 3: In your relationships, did you feel like you lost part of yourself or your identity?

..
____

§ _______________________________________

Question 4: In your relationships, have you felt like your feelings, emotions, and/or responses to situations have been discounted or belittled?

..
____

§ _______________________________________

Question 5: In your relationships, did your significant other apologize when they did something that hurt you, even if it was unintentional?

..
____

§ _______________________________________

Question 6: In your relationships, did your significant other often bash their "crazy ex's"?

..
____

§ _______________________________________

Question 7: In your relationships, did your significant other rely solely on you for entertainment, help, venting, etc or did they have friends to rely on partly too?

..
____

§ _______________________________________

Question 8: In your relationships, did your significant other attempt to or successfully move the relationship forward more quickly than you wanted or were ready for?

..
____

§ _______________________________________

Now that we got through those hard questions, take a minute. Or an hour. Or a day. Take some deep breaths, do some yoga, drink a glass of wine...whatever you need to do to shake off the hugeness of being honest with yourself about what happened in your past relationships. Dealing with the tough things is something we all have to do, but that is when the conscious, deliberate, and intentional act of dating yourself (and of rewiring your brain so that doing something kind for yourself is your first thought when facing difficult things) becomes so important.

Now that you have taken a moment (or several) to take care of yourself, let's discuss why I asked all those tough questions. Those questions all deal with warning signs (we are going to call them red lights) in relationships. Many times, we have difficulty identifying those red lights because we haven't truly identified who we are and how we feel loved. So a controlling significant other can feel like love because we don't know the importance of maintaining our personal identity. I know this book is (mostly) about dating yourself, but the premise of dating yourself is to help you not only keep your cup and bottle full, but to use your new found or rediscovered self-worth to forge and sustain healthy relationships with others too.

That's why I want to take a minute here to make another list; one that's akin to the rainbow picket fence list we made in Chapter 2. But this list is going to apply to other people. I want you to take a minute and think about what you want in relationships, romantic and/or platonic. You're going to list red light personality traits (those things that are an absolute NO in a relationship), yellow light personality traits (those things that one or two might be ok, but 3 or more would definitely combine to make a red light), and green light personality traits (those things that are a must have in your relationships). These green light traits can also bring to light red and yellow light traits, if the green ones are not present. I will give you a few examples from my own list to help you get started.

My Personal Traffic Light List

Red Light Traits	Yellow Light Traits	Green Light Traits
Dishonesty	Job hopping	Compassion
Cheating	Strained relationships with family	Good communicator
Gets angry for small things	No long term relationships	Makes me laugh

Now that you have some ideas of where I want you to go with this, write your own Traffic Light List here. (Definitely add more space if you need…this is an important list!)

Red Light Traits	Yellow Light Traits	Green Light Traits
___________	___________	___________
___________	___________	___________
___________	___________	___________
___________	___________	___________
___________	___________	___________
___________	___________	___________
___________	___________	___________

Now, compare this list to your rainbow picket fence list for yourself. I bet there is some overlap between the who you are now and the yellow light traits and the who you want to be and the green light traits. This correlation between the lists is important. The values, ideals, and traits we hold in high regard for ourselves are often those we look for in others. The struggle in finding that in a partner or friend comes when we are unable to see those positive traits in ourselves. We begin to struggle with our self-worth and then allow others to treat us in ways that are not acceptable. By knowing, naming, and writing those traits that you are working towards and those you already possess, you can begin to increase your self-worth.

This brings us full circle to the WHY regarding continuing to date yourself when you are dating someone else. Dating yourself is so much more than just doing nice things for yourself. It is taking a mindful stance in your brain of prioritizing yourself and your mental health. A relationship, romantic or platonic, where there is no support and respect for the process you are developing to maintain your mental health is never going to be healthy. Read that again if you need. Underline it, highlight it, write it down on a piece of paper and put it on your mirror. Just make sure you understand and remember it.

Once again, I can't tell you what your WHY is for continuing to date yourself when you are dating someone else. But this chapter should have helped you to discover your WHY. Write it here.

Now do something to carry these 2 WHY statements with you; your WHY for dating yourself and your WHY for continuing to date yourself when you are dating someone else. Take a picture on your phone, write it on an index card and put it in your wallet, get creative and type it on a picture you love in a photo editing app. Whatever you need to do to ensure that your WHYS are always with you.

Maybe you've heard the statement that what you surround yourself with is what you will become. That is the reason I want you to carry your WHYS with you. Read them. Multiple times a day. Commit them to memory. Then think about them multiple times a day. Share it with other people if you want to. But make sure that you are frequently and with full belief living, breathing, and focusing on your WHYS.

Listen to Lisa!

When you are really connecting with your Why you will find that things, activities, the way you hold boundaries for yourself, it all becomes non-negotiable. Now that might sound intense but the right partner will honor those non-negotiables and if they don't then you get to say "no" to them and "yes" to someone else.

Making those WHY statements a focus in your life has many benefits. It's one of the ways you begin to retrain your brain. It keeps you honest with yourself about your journey to not only loving, but truly accepting YOU, right where you are. This minute. This second. You can wholeheartedly love and fully accept yourself right now while still working to better yourself. Actually, learning to love and accept yourself where you are is a huge step on the journey to better yourself.

Think about learning to do something you love versus learning to do something you only tolerate. You are going to put so much more time and effort into learning what you love and only a minimal amount of time and effort into learning something you tolerate. The same principle applies to working to better yourself. If you love yourself where you are now, then working to become the person you want to be will develop into a happy habit. If you don't learn to love yourself where you are now, then working to grow into that person you want to become will be a challenging chore.

Your personal WHY'S are so important to this process, but there are also some universal WHY'S regarding the importance of continuing to date yourself while you are dating someone else.

- Learn to appreciate each others differences
- Learn how to find commonality
- Strengthen your ability to compromise
- Become more open minded

We've already done a lot of work to get to the place where you love yourself in this book. But we aren't done yet. And, if I'm being completely honest with you, the process of loving yourself is an ongoing process, but it gets easier and easier.

◆ Ah-Ha! ◆

Chapter 7: What does dating yourself look like when you're dating someone else?

◊ Check In ◊

____

____

____

____

____

We've already talked about why continuing to date yourself when you are in a relationship is important, but now we are going to talk about the more practical side of continuing to date yourself. It may seem, especially in the beginning of a relationship, that taking time for yourself is difficult. The first phase of a relationship is full of wonder and hope and you want to spend every moment possible with the other person. What would happen if you also had those feelings of wonder and hope for your relationship with yourself?

Take a minute and sit with that question. Why don't you have that same wonder and hope for your relationship with yourself? If you have some of the wonder and hope, why don't you have as much? Consider those questions and then do a little free writing next regarding the answers.

To the right person, your need to continue dating yourself will be a positive asset in your relationship. It will enhance your ability to love and your ability to be loved. It will renew your mental capacity and fill your goblet and bottle so that you can continue to give to others.

You may be asking yourself how it works logistically to date yourself when you are dating someone else. I won't lie, it may not be the easiest thing you do. It will take planning and effort. But it is worth it to continue to celebrate you for the amazing woman you are!

The first step to continuing to date yourself when you are dating someone else is to be honest with yourself and the other person. Be honest with yourself about the importance of continuing to date yourself. Keep remembering your WHY. Be honest with yourself about needing the time to refill your goblet and bottle. Remember why keeping your bottle and goblet full are key to you living your most authentic life.

Being honest with the person you are dating is important too. We've discussed several reasons why continuing to date yourself is important in helping you find and maintain a healthy relationship, but it comes more into play here. When you are able to be completely honest with a significant other, which includes sharing your WHY for dating yourself and your plans and date ideas, you allow that person to become part of the journey you are on. Having support on any journey where you are making changes and working to further enhance yourself, your life, and your well-being is indispensable.

We all require accountability. We all crave someone to be our cheerleader. Your significant other should be your biggest cheerleader in this journey. Once you allow them into your expedition party, your significant other can help with accountability. They can not only encourage you to take the time for yourself, but also gift you with opportunities to do so. And by allowing your significant other to join on your expedition party, you may inspire their own journey to find interests and hobbies, or to keep hold of interests and hobbies that they already have.

Let's talk realistically now. Most relationships eventually move towards a co-habitation scenario. And in much of this book, I have talked about the importance of doing things on your own. This concept remains important for your big dates but becomes less important in those everyday dates. It becomes foolish to think about making your significant other leave the house daily for your date time. Good news! They don't have to leave. You can still take a hot bath, go curl up in bed and read a book, or get in the kitchen and bake something while your significant other attends to their own hobbies or interests.

You can even integrate something akin to "parallel play", which is a stage of development for toddlers. The adult version of parallel play would look like this: you and your significant other both engaging in a hobby or interest in the same general location in your house without directly influencing the behavior of the other person. Basically, you would both be doing your own thing and not really interacting much, but still be physically together. Example? Both of you reading books you enjoy on the couch in front of the fireplace on a snowy day.

If you and your partner are able to participate in the adult version of parallel play - we will call it coordinated quiet coexistence (CQC for short), it signifies that you are part of a stable, healthy, and trusting relationship. Attempting the concept of "ignoring each other" in the same room can make your partner feel alone if the trust is not established beforehand. Open communication is key to making this concept part of your relationship with someone else.

Another way to continue dating yourself when you are dating someone else is to schedule activities concurrently that have similar locations. A great example of this would be if your significant other is a golfer and you like to have a drink or two and people watch. While you sit at the bar (or on the patio or wherever) and have your drinks, your significant other can get a round of golf in with their buddies. Side benefit, this also allows you to help your significant other to train themselves to take time to fill their cup.

Now that we have discussed some of the logistics related to continuing to date yourself while you are dating someone else, let's take some time to write down some ways you can accomplish this task! Let's start with things you can do independently at home while your significant other is also at home.

→ _______________________________________

→ _______________________________________

→ _______________________________________

→ _______________________________________

→ _______________________________________

→ _______________________________________

Next, let's find some ideas where CQC can be used.

→ _______________________________________

→ _______________________________________

→ _______________________________________

→ _______________________________________

→ _______________________________________

And now, onwards to ideas where you can plan concurrent activities with your significant other.

→ _________________________________

→ _________________________________

→ _________________________________

→ _________________________________

→ _________________________________

→ _________________________________

Since we have all these fun ideas, now it's time to have a conversation with your significant other about putting some of these into play. Make some time for a date with them. Have an open and honest dialogue with them regarding your NEED to continue dating yourself. Let's chat a little about the emotions that come up when you think about this conversation.

Take a minute, close your eyes, and do four or five 5-5-7 breaths, which are explained below.

Listen to Lisa!

Ah the 557 breath. This is the simplest way to move from the sympathetic nervous system, which is Flight, Fight or Freeze to the parasympathetic which is Rest and Digest. Any time you are feeling stressed your body thinks you are being chased by a bear. It doesn't know that you are just feeling nervous about going out to dinner by yourself. It is such a simple and invisible technique. First take an inhale for a count of 5 and then hold that inhale for a count of 5, then exhale for a count of 7. The longer inhale is the key. That is what tells your brain you are not stressed. Ideally you want to do this 10 times, but I can almost guarantee you will feel a difference after just a couple times.

Now that you have centered yourself, what emotions come up when you are thinking about a discussion with your significant other regarding your need to continue dating yourself? Please feel free to search on the interwebs for feelings chart or feelings wheel to help you with the feelings words if you need! Write down those words here.

<3 _______________________________________

<3 _______________________________________

<3 _______________________________________

<3 _______________________________________

<3 _______________________________________

You may be feeling emotions that you feel are conflicting, and that's ok. Our emotions often seem conflicting, such as when you start a new job. You would likely be feeling excited and nervous at the same time. Many instances of these conflicting emotions are a good example of your critter brain (see chapter 3 if you forget what the critter brain is) attempting to make you think about what's happening. Which is absolutely 100% a healthy element of our brain. The important thing is to be able to differentiate the critter brain emotional response from your authentic emotional response. Then you will be able to process all the emotions in appropriate ways. Below I want you to divide those emotions you wrote above into your critter brain emotions and your authentic emotions.

Critter brain   Authentic

_______________   _______________

_______________   _______________

_______________   _______________

_______________   _______________

_______________   _______________

_______________   _______________

_______________   _______________

Maybe you feel like all your emotions are critter brain emotions or all your emotions are authentic emotions. This is possible, although not likely. Your critter brain is constantly working to protect you, and part of that process is to project emotions that make you pause and think about what is happening or the decision you are making. Your authentic emotions can be similar to your critter brain emotions or completely opposite or somewhere in between, but if you really take a minute and consider the emotions related to the conversation we are discussing, then you will find the divide between these two emotional states.

Below we will discuss each of the largest emotional categories that are listed on the emotions chart and why you may be feeling them related to the conversation with your significant other. Please feel free to add further notes after each emotion.

Proud: Having difficult, or potentially difficult, discussions with a significant other can be a definitive source of pride. Also, standing up for your desires and needs can be a source of pride.

Joyful: Finding the strength to put yourself first can provide significant joy.

Intrigued: This emotion can be evoked during a conversation like this when your significant other provides ideas or insight into helping with your journey.

Trusting: This can be provided when your significant other provides a safe environment for you to have conversations like this.

Loving: I'm leaving this one up to you…. You have already discovered how you feel loved and I trust that you can determine how this emotion can come up during and after this conversation.

Peaceful: This emotion could present especially after this conversation, when you have a moment to reflect on the outcome of the conversation.

Ashamed: This emotion can come up if you have struggled with self-care and self-love in the past.

Sad: This emotion may present if the outcome of the conversation is not what you expected.

Surprised: As above, this emotion may present if
the outcome of the conversation is not what you expected.

____

____

____

____

____

Afraid: Again, this emotion may present if the
outcome of the conversation is not what you expected.

____

____

____

____

____

Disgusted: And yet again, this emotion may present if the outcome of the conversation is not what you expected.

Angry: This emotion may be evoked if the conversation goes awry with no expectation of being able to fix it.

Now that we have really examined these emotions, you may need to take some time before you move on. Use some of your little date ideas, do some self-care. Take some family time. Phone a friend. Making sure you take time to feel and sit with your emotion is incredibly important, but can have distinctive fall out. So taking some time to step back from the emotions and do something for you is just as important.

Wrapping up this conversation about how you continue to date yourself when you are dating someone else, I want to go back to that big word, WHY. Your personal why for dating yourself and your why for continuing to date yourself once you are dating someone else. Go ahead and write those down here again.

Why I'm dating myself:

Why am I continuing to date myself even when I'm dating someone else:

____

____

____

____

Now I want to add another why. What would it mean to you if you are able to accomplish this dating yourself thing? Not only accomplish it, but really stick to it and make it a regular part of your life?

____

____

____

____

How would it change your life?

____

____

____

____

____

Now, how would it change the lives of those around you? Significant other, kids, friends, family, co-workers....

____

____

____

____

I want you to use how impactful you could be on others in your life to write another why. There are times when holding on to how changes can affect others in your life can be the deciding factor between sticking to your resolve or not. I am not saying you should make changes for others, the desire to change should always come from inside you, but there are times when your personal why may not seem good enough. Part of this journey is helping you discover that your personal why is ALWAYS enough. However, there are times when an external why can be extremely beneficial. Write that external why here.

Now I want you to take a piece of paper or index cards and write your whys on each one. You will have 3 why statements. Put them in your wallet. Take a picture of them on your phone and favorite it. Just be sure you have access to them ALL THE TIME. Hold on to your whys. Do the same thing with your anchors from the chart in chapter 5. Write them down. Carry them with you, either physically or a picture on your phone. Be sure you always have access to the reason you want to make change (your whys) and the things that help you stabilize through a storm and a celebration (your anchors). The process of learning to date yourself won't always be easy and these statements will help see you through the tough times.

But, and this is a big but (and I cannot lie), these why statements and anchors are just as important when you are celebrating your wins. Let's sit with that for a minute. Why would you need your whys and anchors when you are celebrating wins? First, let's examine the why part. Your why keeps you connected to the reason you started this crazy journey with me. But it also keeps you connected to the 'why behind the why' - which I will let Lisa explain.

Listen to Lisa!

When you connect to your "Why" when things are going well it feels great. You get to integrate why you wanted to do this in the first place and now look how well it is going for you. I like to use anchors for both rough roads and celebration. Dance it off or Dance it out! (If music and dancing are your anchors, like mine.)

So, continuing to connect to all those meaningful whys remains paramount throughout this entire expedition (which really doesn't end when this book ends…but we will address that later). Continuing on to your anchors, the easiest way to explain the relevance of keeping them close during your wins is this. When on a boat, you anchor it during a storm (when things get tough during your journey of growth). However, you also anchor a boat to have some drinks, go fishing, and do all kinds of other fun things! So, clinging to those anchors during the difficult growth and the celebrations full of elation the way a boat clings to its anchor will help you to stay connected to your deepest why.

◆ Ah-Ha! ◆

Chapter 8: How long do I have to date myself?

Short answer, forever. Long answer – SURPRISE – it's the same!! This chapter doesn't end here, however. Even with a short answer to this chapter's question, there is so much more to discuss. You may be thinking, "well, duh". Or you may be thinking, "This lady is nuts"! Or a million other thoughts may be crossing your mind. So why (that word comes up an awful lot, doesn't it??) do we need to discuss the relatively short answer to this chapters' question? Because it is imperative to have a realistic idea of the journey you are on, especially once you reach the last pages of this book. I refuse to call it the end of the book because I honestly believe this book does not end. It can be worked through again and again, to solidify your why, process the act of dating yourself during different phases of your life, discover new ideas for dating yourself and you experience more/gain different interests and hobbies/move to new places/have financial changes and a million others things that can happen and cause you to refine and/or add and subtract things from your personal identity.

Your personal identity is very fluid, as we discussed in Chapter 1. Your core beliefs, principles, and values probably won't make huge shifts (although they can, and that is 1000% ok), but your habits, dreams, goals, talents, and interests will evolve over time. That is a huge part of why I structured this book the way I did. I wanted you to be able to work through it again and again as you need and desire. Continuing to advance, cultivate, and expand your personal identity is fundamental to growth in your life. Remaining stagnant in any area of your life will lead to despondency and melancholy in other areas very quickly - and please notice I used the word WILL, not might, not could, not possibly, because there is no question that stagnation in one area greatly affects every area of your life.

Preventing stagnation is a huge reason why dating yourself is a life-long endeavor. Continuing to identify and develop new areas in your personal identity is another reason why you should continue dating yourself. Many times we discover new dreams and goals as we work toward current ones. This usually leads to developing new habits, interests, and talents. All of these expansions, augmentations, and progressions to your personal identity can create changes in every area we explore in this book. Therefore, your ideas related to dating yourself can, will, and should shift as you continue to step forward (wearing kick ass shoes) in life.

Why else is continuing to date yourself forever important? IT'S FUN!!! I hope you have discovered by this point in the book how fun it is to plan and implement these ideas to date yourself. If you haven't, I recommend going back to Chapter 1 and working through it again. There are multiple studies that show regular self-care (i.e. DATING

YOURSELF) has huge benefits for mental, physical, and spiritual health.

The benefits of self-care can impact stress reduction, minimization of depression and anxiety symptoms, making concentration and focus easier, lessening frustrations, improve connections with others, and increase positive energy and happiness.

Dating yourself is self-care. But it's also more than that. It is intentional, deliberate, and purposeful discovery of your identity. It's conscious effort to keep your goblet and bottle full. It's a drive to create a strength in yourself so you are able to develop and commit to boundaries. The idea of dating yourself is so all encompassing that it is truly difficult to describe in a sentence. Or two. But it absolutely includes self-care.

Let's talk about some of the benefits you want to see from dating yourself! Try to get 6-8 of each of these benefits!

Physical benefits

Mental benefits

Spiritual benefits

Now, I want to address how these benefits would change your life. After all, this book is about change! Take each of the benefits you listed above and really think about how it would effect your every day. You may not have all the blanks above filled in. You may have more than than would fit in those blanks. That's why there is a lot of white space in this book. And why I encourage you to add more space if you need.

Physical benefit   Effect on your life

Mental benefit

Effect on your life

Spiritual benefit   Effect on your life

Now, I want you to put this book down for a bit. Maybe an hour feels right to you, maybe a day, maybe somewhere in between. Just step away for a bit. Find some sunshine and recharge!

Welcome back! I hope you had a refreshing recharge. I wanted you to step away for a bit to really process the last lists we made. That was some heavy stuff and considering the benefits of performing self-care, or maybe the lack of such benefits you are experiencing right now, can really jumble things up in your brain. I wanted you to be clear for this next step and to be able to step outside your head and gain some perspective.

Go back and look at the lists you made of physical, mental, and spiritual benefits of actively and regularly participating in self-care. I want you to pick two out of each section, one that you feel is most important to YOU and the other that you feel is most important to an external motivator, such as a child, parent, SO, etc. Put a star next to those two in each section. We will come back to those in a bit.

Consider the rainbow picket fence version of you we discussed earlier in Chapter 2. Do the ways your life would be affected correlate in any way to that version of you? Do you see how the benefits of self-care and dating yourself would contribute to building this version of yourself? Building this rainbow picket fence version of yourself is much like building a house. You start with a blueprint, pour the foundation, build the skeleton, put on the roof, add the windows and doors, and then do the finishing work.

Building the rainbow picket fence version of you works the same way. You start with a blueprint (that rainbow picket fence version of you), pour the foundation (develop your personal identity), build the skeleton (identify the ways you can date yourself), put on the roof (identifying your anchors), add windows and doors (boundary setting), and finishing work (putting all these things into play and start DATING YOURSELF!!!)

As with building a house, the blueprint you are working from may change as things in your life shift. Thankfully, it is nowhere near as monetarily expensive to reconstruct yourself or to change your blueprint in the middle of the build! We will continue this discussion in Chapter 10.

◆ Ah-Ha! ◆

Chapter 9: What if I get tired of myself?

____

____

____

____

____

What if you get tired of yourself? Short answer, you will. And that is when dating yourself becomes the most important. When you feel like someone else is getting tired of you, the general response is to do something nice for them. So continuing to date yourself through the "tired phase" is critical. This would be a great time to pull out a really big Big Date idea! Take yourself away for a weekend or a week. Revamp your wardrobe or bedroom. Just don't give up!

We all know that we get tired of other people - movies are the only place where people want to be together all the time. Needing a break from someone doesn't mean you love them any less, it means you are human. Similarly, getting tired of dating yourself doesn't mean that you love yourself any less. Rather, it means that you have been doing an amazing job of consistently and intentionally spending time with yourself.

Let me back up. When you are taking care of others, be it at home, work, with friends, your mind is not actively in a place where you are spending time with you. You are too concerned with external factors to be in the moment enjoying your own company. This is the same reason why other relationship experts will tell you to schedule date nights with your significant other because doing regular weekly events and chores don't provide the same benefit of scheduled, intentional time.

So, in order to get tired of yourself, you have to be scheduling that consistent time where you are honestly sitting with yourself. Kudos to you for getting to this point! That's where the benefit of the big date idea comes in. Just like in dates with another person, we can get stuck in a rut dating ourselves. Changing things up some, getting out of the town where you live, or finding a new adventure can reset your mind and help you get over the "I'm sick of me" slump.

This is also where that little card where you wrote your WHY'S and anchors becomes important. Rereading those whys and holding on to those anchors will help you reconnect with the reasons you started this process and the big picture of what you want to get out of it. This is also the time to reach out to those people you listed in Chapter 4 on your accountability list! They can help to solidify your whys, but at this point in the process, they can probably share some of the positive changes they have watched unfold in your life!

Speaking from a clinical standpoint regarding making significant psychological changes, oftentimes having the knowledge beforehand that difficulty will present itself on the journey can alleviate some of the frustrations along the way. Struggles will surface on this journey. It is not a question of IF, but a question of WHEN. However, preparation will allow you to view those struggles as an opportunity rather than a roadblock.

I want to start by addressing the struggles that I personally experienced, as well as struggles that others shared with me. In an effort to be completely candid, the struggles that were shared with me by friends were experienced while they took a similar journey to the one you are on now; however, they did not have this book to accompany them on that journey. I will add that my part on their journeys was a huge part of my why in writing this book.

Back to the struggles you may come across. I want to first address those struggles, and then we will discuss how to conquer them, since the conquering of those struggles is more personal than the struggles themselves. This is a fairly universal concept. You will often find others who have dealt with similar struggles as you. The variant will come in how they were able to overcome those struggles. It may take you time to discover the best way for you to move past the roadblocks you come across. AND THAT'S OK. Greatness takes time. And effort. And failure. Just keep reminding yourself that you are worth it. And let Lisa and I believe in you until you can believe in yourself.

Listen to Lisa!

There is a saying "Small hinges swing BIG doors" which means that every little thing you do will get you that much closer to your goal. If you are in a rut, go back to basics, and refresh with those small things that make you feel like you are doing something. Buy yourself some flowers, turn the notifications off on your phone and just listen to music, take a bath. All of it counts and always remember to celebrate along the way.

The first struggle is time. I have thought to myself, many times, when it came to a scheduled self-date, "I don't have time for this today". I would think about the other things on my to-do list, the laundry, the dishes, the grocery shopping. And then I would try to push myself and my mental health and my identity to the bottom of that list. This may be one of the behaviors or attitudes that led to disassociation with your self-identity and unintentional self-sabotage.

The concept of self-sacrifice for those you love is rampant in our culture. And it is also COMPLETELY WRONG. You absolutely, completely, 1000% CANNOT be what you want and need to be for others unless you are taking care of yourself. We discussed this in Chapter 4 with the concept of the bottle and goblet.

The next struggle is resources, other than time. It can be a struggle to allocate money, space, or other finite resources to the concepts of self-care, self-discovery, and self-love. Remember, we discussed both large and small date ideas earlier. We also talked about getting other people involved in this process of finding your identity.

The final common struggle I have encountered is guilt. You may think that guilt directly ties into the time and resources mentioned above, and it can, but more often than not, the guilt is a separate entity attempting to sabotage your journey of self-discovery. Here is a real life, real time example of guilt that is not tied to time or other resources.

I am currently sitting in a Bdubs writing this chapter. I don't have any other expectations on my time this afternoon. Actually, I was told by more than one close person in my life that I needed to take a few hours out of the house to finish writing today. The expense of my food (and let's be honest, beer) is not a concern. But I still have been struggling with the guilt of sitting here, writing and sharing my story, while there are things to be done at home. I'm struggling with spending money on my lunch when I could be using that $30 to do something else unrelated to self-care.

Instead of wallowing in that guilt, or allowing myself to create excuses, I am churning out words and attempting to make them make sense. How did I get past the excuses and the guilt? Let's explore that next.

When we look at the issue of time, and feeling unable to take time for a you date, one of the easiest ways I have found to move past this issue is to get permission from someone you are close to in your life. This may seem counter intuitive, but in reality, this is called third party validation. If we look at your authentic brain as one person and your critter brain as another, you are basically attempting to "sell" to your critter brain the importance of taking time to date yourself.

When you gain permission from someone else, the third party, it provides validation to your critter brain that not only is the time to date yourself essential, but it is also a logical and credible use of your time. The third party is not actually granting that permission (if you feel that your third party can actually grant you permission to take time for yourself, or that you need their permission to take time for yourself, that is another issue we need to address - and I will in Appendix B). What "asking" permission from a third party does is it takes the decision out of your hands and out of the reach of your critter brain.

Suddenly, your critter brain is on board with taking this time out for yourself. The act of gaining that validation from a third party allows your critter brain to look at the situation from a new vantage point because the third party also has your best interest and protection in mind. Having this third party validation allows the critter brain to calm down enough to consider that maybe taking some time out for yourself is a good idea.

The second issue to overcome is the value you place on resources other than time, such as financial resources, space in your home, and/or space away from friends, family, pets, chores, etc. There are multiple ways to address and overcome these issues.

Regarding financial resources, there are multiple date ideas that do not cost a lot financially. Taking a color walk (finding things in nature that match different colors and taking pictures of them), making a picnic for yourself, hiking and taking wildlife and nature photos, going for coffee and people watching, heading to the library or bookstore to sit and read; these are all fantastic date ideas that have minimal financial involvement. If you start with dates that have smaller financial involvement, then the object of space in your home will not be an issue.

However, if there are reasons (and believe me, there are many good ones) for needing date ideas that are more homebound, finding that space can be difficult. Creativity in both using space and hobby date ideas is key if this is what you need. I have multiple areas of my house where I have placed a random bookshelf that if filled with hobby materials, such as yarn to crochet, painting supplies, and card making supplies. All those supplies are in easy to move totes that I can easily take to the dining room table and use then pick up without issue.

Another way to overcome the financial barrier is to ask others for "pre-paid dates" for gift giving holidays. I love to suggest this to other women because it often breaks the financial barrier and the next barrier of guilt, since the date was provided by someone else. When someone else provides the financial backing for a date, suddenly the guilt of wasting their money and not using the date outweighs the guilt related to dating yourself.

Another way to overcome the self-sabotage guilt is to JUST MAKE IT HAPPEN! Look at your whys. Remember where you were at the start of this journey. Find positive replacement statements that directly contrast the guilt statement. Then keep repeating those statements until you forget to feel the guilt. But don't stop dating yourself in the meantime....working through the guilt is two-pronged; the action and the replacement statements. Let's look at some examples of replacement statements regarding self-sabotage guilt.

My Guilt Statements:	My Replacement Statements:
** It doesn't matter if do this today, I can still be 100% for my family tonight.	I will be my best self if I take this time regularly, not just when I think I need it.
** If I stay home, I can get ahead on my house-work and that will help my mental health.	The housework I need to do will still be there when I get done with my date and my mental health will already be protected.
** It doesn't matter if I really do these dates because I don't think it will have the effect that this dating yourself idea promises.	I am WORTH the time, energy, and space to discover who I am, who I want to be, and to travel the road to bring me to that person.

Now, let's explore some of your guilt statements versus the replacement statements you can find to help move forward and leave that guilt in the dust!

Your Guilt Statements: Your Replacement Statements:

** ____________________   ____________________

____________________   ____________________

____________________   ____________________

____________________   ____________________

____________________   ____________________

** ____________________   ____________________

____________________   ____________________

____________________   ____________________

____________________   ____________________

** ____________________   ____________________

____________________   ____________________

____________________   ____________________

____________________   ____________________

____________________   ____________________

** ____________________   ____________________

____________________   ____________________

**

**

**

♦ Ah-Ha! ♦

Chapter 10: I now pronounce you yourself and yourself!

◊ Check In ◊

____

____

____

____

____

You made it!! You are now dating yourself, and, I'm hoping, happy in the process! Reaching this point in the book calls for celebration! Crack open a bottle and have a drink! Toast yourself and the journey you are on! (This would also be a great time to pull out a big date idea to celebrate!)

However, this is just the beginning. We have already discussed why continuing to date yourself is important, but what happens if you start to get lax and you aren't doing what you know you need to? You get this book off the coffee table, where you keep it because you love it so much (or - let's be realistic, if you are anything like me - dig it off the overcrowded bookshelf where it sits between that novel you bought 3 months ago and haven't cracked open yet and the poetry book you wrote in 8th grade) and work through it again.

Here's a secret though…you don't have to work through it in order this time. Wait…what? "But don't I need to go through the same process again?" No, you don't. You put in the work and built the foundation. You can easily renovate what sits on top of that foundation, room by room, or chapter by chapter, but there isn't an order that must be followed. Use your intuition. Just open the book to a page and start working through it again. Add more paper. Color out what doesn't work for you any more and add new. Just make sure you are continually evaluating where you are in the process and holding yourself accountable for continuing to date yourself.

This chapter is going to draw on a lot of the previous chapters in the book, and require a fair amount of transcription from those chapters so we can further explore some of these ideas and continue to compound and add to how they affect your relationship with yourself and continuing to date yourself - FOR THE REST OF YOUR LIFE!! (If you are like me, taking a picture of the information to transcribe with your smart phone so you don't have to flip back and forth will be your best friend in this situation.)

Let's first explore your whys. All 3 of them were compiled in chapter 7. Let's put them here again.

Why I'm dating myself:

Why am I continuing to date myself even when I am dating someone else:

External why:

Now, let's head back to chapter 6 and look at your traffic light traits. I want you to choose the two most important red, yellow and green light traits from your list and write them here.

Red Light: Yellow Light: Green Light:

________________   ________________   ____________

________________   ________________   ____________

These two things, the traffic light traits and your 3 why's, may not seem to have a super direct correlation, but they do. Losing your identity isn't necessarily or inherently or directly related to being in a toxic or abusive relationship. But it generally does follow leaving a toxic or abusive relationship, whether it is a romantic, platonic, or familial relationship. More importantly, losing your identity is almost always associated with a toxic self relationship or self-image. These toxic relationships, whether internal or external, are what help to determine both our traffic light traits and our why's.

These relationship experiences also help to shape that rainbow picket fence version of yourself, which is a large part of what we have been working toward throughout this whole book. Looking back at those traffic light traits, I want you to think about a specific instance that led you to realize each of those traffic light traits you listed on this page were the most important. Be sure to be as specific as possible and engage all 5 senses in writing down the examples you are depicting next.

Red Light Trait 1(RLT1): __________________________

Specific instance: (engage all 5 senses in your description)

Red Light Trait 2 (RLT2): ____________________________

Specific instance: (engage all 5 senses in your description)

Yellow Light Trait 1 (YLT1): _______________________________

Specific instance: (engage all 5 senses in your description)

____

____

____

____

Yellow Light Trait 2 (YLT2): _______________________________

Specific instance: (engage all 5 senses in your description)

____

____

____

____

Green Light Trait 1 (GLT1): _________________________

Specific instance: (engage all 5 senses in your description)

____

____

____

____

Green Light Trait 2 (GLT2): _________________________

Specific instance: (engage all 5 senses in your description)

____

____

____

____

Why are we looking at these specific examples? There are several reasons. One, exploring the why of anything can help to solidify the lessons learned and to retain those lessons in a meaningful way. Second, identifying those specific instances and engaging all the senses when identifying them is helpful in relating the instance to current feelings and situations. Forming the relationship between past lessons and current situations allows the brain to retrain itself to seek out or ignore people and situations that bring about those strong feelings. This is how you train your brain (both the critter brain and the authentic brain) to put your mental health, your needs, and your relationship with yourself as a priority.

I want you to now take your thoughts on the traffic light traits and their related, specific instances a step further. I want you to take each of those traits and, after thinking about the specific instance related to it, write down your current feelings about that trait and the instance you described.

Current Feelings:

RLT1:

RLT1 instance:

RLT2:

RLT2 instance:

YLT1:

YLT1 instance:

YLT2:

YLT2 instance:

GLT1:

GLT1 instance:

GLT2:

GLT2 instance:

Making time to reflect on the happenings that brought importance to those traits and the current feelings that you possess when sitting with both is important to maintaining the relationship you are building with yourself. Including time to sit with feelings is always essential (I schedule time at the beginning and end of my day to do so), but when those feelings are attached to a key piece of your puzzle - your traffic light traits - it becomes even more critical to not only sit with them, but to process them and the importance they hold in the puzzle.

Allowing yourself this time to determine where those traits became important, to allow yourself to feel and process the event that made them important, and then taking the power you gained from that event to help you shape the life you want to develop is a very important part of this journey you are on.

By the way, SURPRISE, you absolutely did gain power from those instances. YOU ARE STILL HERE. You are CONSCIENTIOUSLY and CONSISTENTLY moving toward the life you both want and deserve. And you now recognize that you do, in fact, deserve a wonderful, beautiful, crazy, exciting, (insert more adjectives to describe your new life here) ____________________

____

____________________________ life.

     Now, I want to continue our discussion about stagnation. We all know it happens. It is usually unintentional, and with a little bit of forward thinking, you can avoid it in your relationship with yourself.

     Take a minute and go back to Chapter 8 where we discussed the benefits that you are looking to gain from dating yourself and practicing high level self care. I want you to write them down here also so you can easily reference them throughout the next part of this chapter.

Physical benefits

Mental benefits

Spiritual benefits

These benefits are part of your roadmap to the relationship you want with yourself and the life you want to live. But they can also be a roadmap to date ideas that you have not considered. You may be questioning my sanity still, although if you have made it this far in the book, I hope you see the method behind my madness.

Here is an example from my life for how I used the benefits I see and continue to want to see from dating myself to help me find new date ideas. For me, a huge physical benefit of dating myself is working to lessen the frequency of my hemiplegic migraines. How can the idea of lessening the frequency of my hemiplegic migraines bring me new ideas for dates? I've spent many hours reading about new ways to help prevent migraines and discussed them with my medical team. Then I have parlayed those ideas into dates. I took a cooking class to help me learn how to cook with my new dietary restrictions. I got cryotherapy and then went for a walk. I treated myself to massages.

One of the biggest mental health benefits that I am always continuing to work on is maintaining my stress at the lowest level possible. I schedule "nothing days" where I get a whole day to do whatever I want….no housework, laundry, cooking, cleaning, working, or writing allowed. I get a manicure and pedicure every 2 weeks (done by a good friend who understands that my mani/pedi time is a stress preventer and a self-date). I go for long walks with my best girl (my Dachshund Daisy Mae) and listen to music or podcasts. I bake - a lot!

This is one of my favorites! One of the spiritual benefits that I noticed while I was dating myself was mindfulness. I was more mindful of my body, my thoughts, my emotions, and my relationships. To help maintain and expand my mindfulness, I have made daily yoga and meditation dates with myself a priority. I spend at least an hour each day working on my mindfulness. It has made all my other benefits much more noticeable!

Now I want you to use the benefits you have listed to develop some new, unique date ideas!

Physical Benefit   New Date Idea

__________________   __________________________

                                    ____

                                    ____

                                    ____

                                    ____

Physical Benefit   New Date Idea

__________________   __________________________

                                    ____

                                    ____

                                    ____

Physical Benefit   New Date Idea

__________________   __________________________

                                    ____

                                    ____

Physical Benefit

New Date Idea

Physical Benefit

New Date Idea

Physical Benefit

New Date Idea

Mental Benefit   New Date Idea

_______________   _________________________________

                              ____

                              ____

                              ____

Mental Benefit   New Date Idea

_______________   _________________________________

                              ____

                              ____

                              ____

Mental Benefit   New Date Idea

_______________   _________________________________

                              ____

                              ____

                              ____

Mental Benefit   New Date Idea

_______________   _________________________________

Mental Benefit

New Date Idea

Mental Benefit

New Date Idea

Spiritual Benefit

New Date Idea

Spiritual Benefit

New Date Idea

Spiritual Benefit

New Date Idea

Spiritual Benefit

New Date Idea

Spiritual Benefit New Date Idea

_________________ _____________________________

 ____

 ____

 ____

Spiritual Benefit New Date Idea

_________________ _____________________________

 ____

 ____

 ____

 ____

NOW PUT THOSE NEW DATE IDEAS INTO PLAY!!!
Have fun. Be authentically, unapologetically, magically,
beautifully YOU!!!!

   CONGRATULATIONS!! You have successfully
completed round one in this book and the process of
dating yourself! Always remember, on an airplane they tell
you to put your mask on before you help someone else put
their mask on. Keep that attitude for the rest of your life.
Read this next sentence over and over. Commit it to
memory.

YOU CAN NOT BE EVERYTHING TO EVERYONE. BUT YOU CAN BE EVERYTHING TO ONE PERSON....

YOURSELF.

Other people in your life have more than one person helping them. They have a support system other than you. Most women refuse to rely on other support, which is why you HAVE to put yourself first. You have to be sure you take time to fill that bottle and goblet. And when you start to question if you are making the right moves, doing the right thing, come back and read chapters again. Find your why. Reconnect with it. Remember that "NO" is a complete sentence.

Then keep moving forward and dating the most wonderful, beautiful, special, unique, amazing, extraordinary, marvelous person......YOU!!!

♦Ah-Ha!♦

____

____

____

____

____

End note.

Please, please reach out to someone. The world needs you.

If you are experiencing domestic violence, please reach out to someone who can help. Call 1-800-799-7233 or text START to 88788.

If you are experiencing thoughts of self-harm or suicide, please reach out to someone who can help. Call 988 or text 988.